THE LIGHT'S ON, BUT NO ONE'S HOME

FROM THE SAME AUTHOR

French books only

ULTIMA VERITAS
lulu.com, 2013

CODEX LETHALIS
Hachette Black Moon, 2013

L'AXE DU SANG
MA Editions, 2014

BUSHIDO
Fortuna Editions, 2015

BUSHIDO 2
Fortuna Editions, 2016

BUSHIDO 3
Fortuna Editions, 2016

L'EQUATION DE L'ESPOIR
Futur Antérieur Editions, 2022

PYT

THE LIGHT'S ON,
BUT NO ONE'S HOME

A huge thank you to Ayla for the translation
from french to english

ILLUSTRATIONS OF HUMAN NATURE

fa

FUTUR ANTERIEUR
éditions

Futur Antérieur Éditions is not a legal entity, it is a fancy name created by the
author for communication purposes.

Info & orders: pluscontumeurs.com (french & english website)

ISBN: 978-2-9550128-3-3

All the illustrations published in my previous book
The Equation of Hope
(L'Équation de l'Espoir, in french only)

«Our species does not have
the profile to face itself»

«I bought a book about memory,
but I forgot where I put it»

AMNESIA GENERATING CONSTANCY

«If justice is blindfolded, then freedom is wedged»

FREE TO BE ADDICTED

«While the North is sorting, the South is dealing»

JOHN, DON'T FORGET TO PUT THE CANS IN THE RECYCLING BIN!
MOUSSA, DON'T FORGET TO GO TO THE LANDFILL TO COLLECT THE CANS!
Pyt 22
SORT YOUR CONSCIOUSNESS BEFORE YOUR SCRAPS

«When your tsunami will stop me to watch Netflix,
we'll advise»

EQUAL EGOS

«Please do not create unnecessary panic by shouting
« Fire! » unless you are yourself set ablaze»

THE METAPHOR OF THE CONFLAGRATION

«I'm gonna show you how doing nothing
can still cause a reaction»

FREE IN OUR DENIAL

"Collective awareness won't take place tonight,
due to individual protests"

HARMONIOUS MESS

21

"The production/consumption couple is about to divorce, but it is already fighting for child custody»

ON THE ROAD TO ESCAPE

"The road of human rights ends at the end of my field,
after that it's no longer my home»

THE BALANCE OF SUFFERING

«What should a teacher think about his class,
which has been fucking everything up for
more than two thousand years?»

CULT SEQUENCE

«Diving in our inner self is taking the risk
to come back with company»

THE CHOICE TO NOT CHOOSE

«No, it's not a contemporary musical piece sir,
but an alarm»

AFTER ME, THE FLOOD

«The pain of living combined with the sorrow of dying
is an appalling pairing»

BLUES

«I believe thus you're following me»

BAD FAITH

«I don't want to live after my death,
it already pissed me off enough»

LIFE AFTER LIFE

«Why me?»

STATE OF THE MIND

«The sense of humor is not a path,
but a state of the mind»

JOKE ASIDE

«We got the wrong idols»

MISPLACED DEVOTION

«Inappropriate marriage of convenience»

«This dead end is absolutely and perfectly boring»

THE DEADLY BEAUTY OF IMPERFECTION

«As long as we think that time is money,
we won't get any benefit out of it»

CARPE DIEM

«I'm powering my bad faith with sun's energy,
so it's doubly free»

CHANGE WITHOUT CHANGING

51

«I don't even wish to want anymore»

DECAY OF EFFORT

Occidental proverb

«As long as I eat, you are fasting»

BALANCE OF IMBALANCE

«Developing countries in a dead-end path of development»

INAPPROPRIATE QUESTION

«When the interstellar void makes fun
of the one in my fridge»

THE CONQUEST OF THE VOID

«If hope dies last, we should catch it very quickly before it's the last thing left"

A BOTTLE IN THE SEA

«If we knew we held the universal record for bullshit,
we would have been even prouder of ourselves»

TOP OF THE CLASS

«When we choose to skip the question,
it is no wonder that the answer ignores us»

UNWANTED REFLECTIONS

«Scorched earth will always be useful
to rekindle the barbecue of our desires»

«Do as I say and above all,
don't do to me what I did to you»

CAUSE OF WAR

«Take the opportunity before
she takes advantage of you»

WITH FULL CONSCIOUSNESS

"This stretch of highway was so long it seemed free,
but I think I can see a huge toll station in
the distance. I feel like we're going to be busted»

QUIZ OF THE CENTURY

«Even if you knew, you wouldn't believe it, trust me!»

«Progress is the future, but it's not necessarily a present»

«The wild beast embodied by our instincts will only submit by force, so it is useless to give it a bunch of flowers and a chocolate box»

«Killing the difference to be sure to remain the same»

SIMILAR, BUT NOT THE SAME

«The mankind has no equal, because its ego does not know the meaning of this word»

WEAK PATRIARCHY

«I'll show you my screen only if you show me yours»

TO BE OR NOT TO BE... CONNECTED

85

«You may be fat but I still find you bio-tiful»

MAINTAINED FAT

«Thank you for keeping the war going to allow me to satisfy my own hunger»

«I want to know, but the truth doesn't interest me»

THE KNOWLEDGE OF IGNORANCE

«At least we'll die clean and healthy»

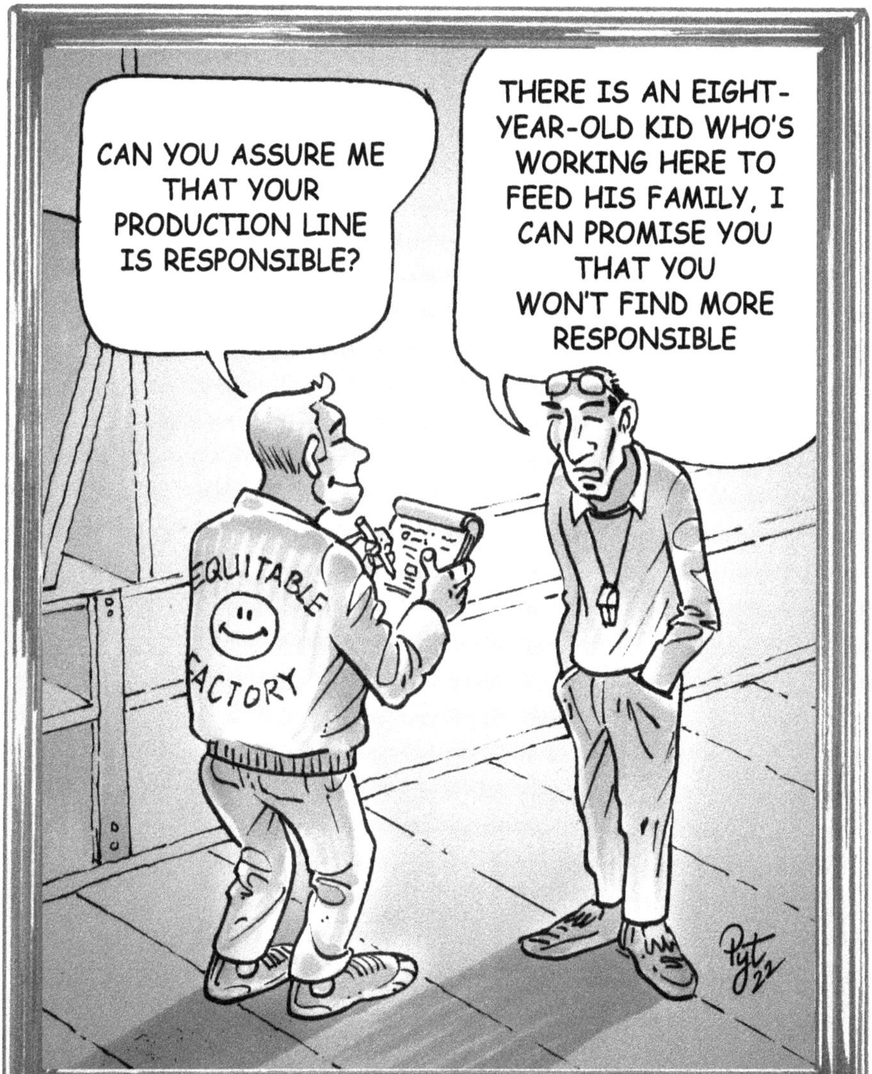

MORE OR LESS FAIR

«To say that growth is a dead end
is the yardstick of understatement

THE GROWTH OF DISDAIN

"Will our future tell us a little more about our past?

NO FUTURE

«Fashion is seductive, but seduction is oldfashioned»

MAKE AN IMPRESSION

«Everytime I lend my voice,
I feel like I lose my words a little more»

DID SOMEBODY SAY CYNIC?

«It is possible to get around the law,
but you must take the routes provided for this purpose»

THE ECONOMY OF ADDICTION

«She was so brilliant that she was elected
as the man of the century»»

BECAUSE THEY ARE NOT WORTH

«This vaccine piques my curiosity while triggering a certain suspicion in me and I was perfectly right»

Aryan existential question

«Should we molt to become less stupid?»

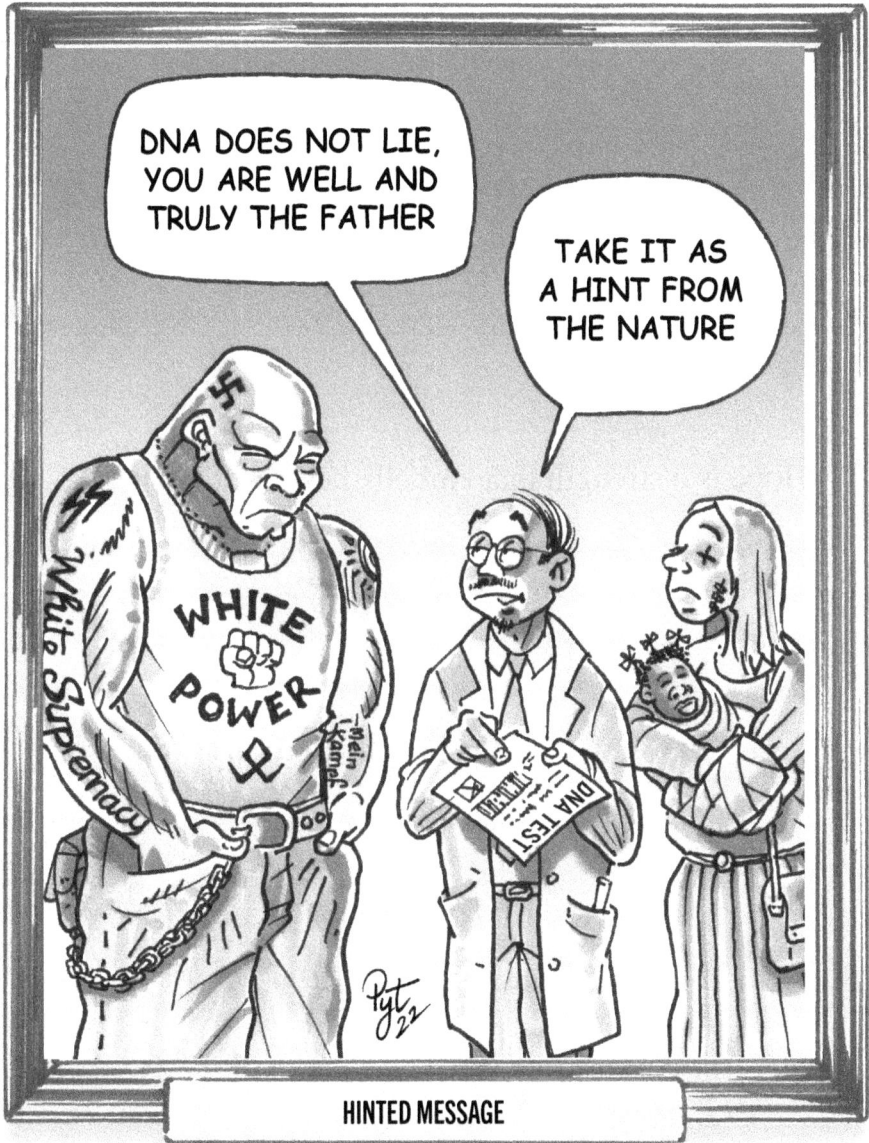

HINTED MESSAGE

«Hope is a strength that embellishes our weaknesses»

THE POWER OF HOPE

«I don't know what you're talking about,
but I'll give you my opinion anyway»

I NEED A SHEPHERD

«I'd much rather bury myself alive than die outdoors»

RABBIT HOLE FOR EARTHLINGS

«Do not confuse blues and spiritual gloom,
although both define the colors of our days»

DEATH IN THE SOUL

«I have the best reasons to believe that I am right.
That's why I have peace of mind»

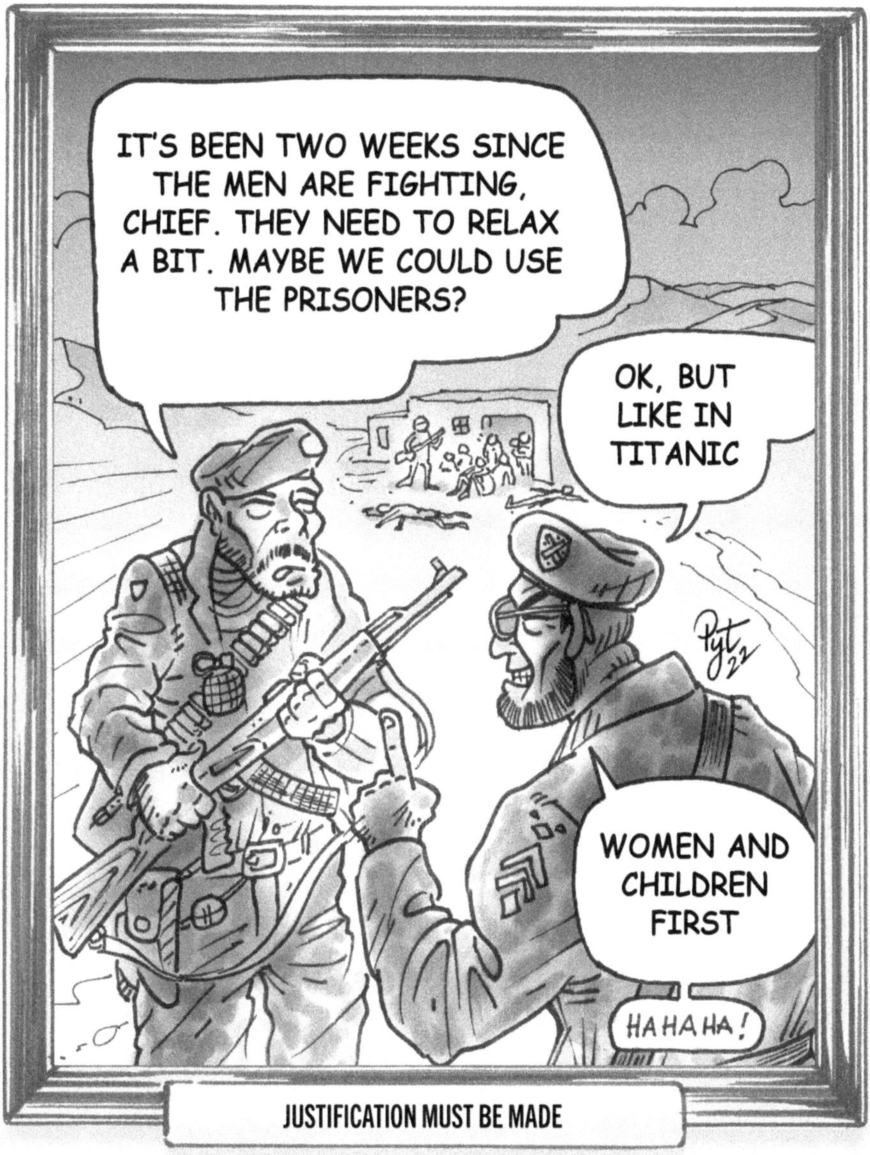

JUSTIFICATION MUST BE MADE

«In ballistics, do not confuse asshole with exit opening»

ANUS HORIBILIS

«We can't do it again today,
but maybe it was possible yesterday»

THE TEACHING OF DENIAL

"The opportunity was too good for me.
So I fucked up»

OPPORTUNITY MAKES THE THIEF

«Clothes don't make the man,
but to be safe, I shot him anyway»

I SEE, THEREFORE I JUDGE

«Money is not food, but it is quite useful to starve»

MY PRECIOUS

«The future is a challenge that our rotten past wasn't able
to conjugate in the present tense»

THE SLIPPERY SLOPE OF ARROGANCE

«We take the same ones and start again»

COMMUNAL UTOPIAS

«Mom, I would like a goldfish,
but from the Findus for Kids species»

GLOBAL VIRUS

Notice to the participants

«For the sake of common sense,
please do not turn the light on when a blind person
is doing his obstacle race»

«When mankind will have got rid of its own impulses,
there won't be much left of itself»

MINE'S BIGGER THAN YOURS

« I do not even think about it, but I'll do it anyway»

SYMPHONY OF UNCONSCIOUSNESS

«If I don't watch the wave that's crashing into me,
maybe she will avoid me?»

HOIST BY ONE'S OWN PETARD

«I chose to build to become,
rather than becoming someone to then build myself»

THE EMPTINESS OF PRIDE

«The patience of emotions»

«The soul is a hypothesis
that hope turns into a likely certainty»

MOODS

«Despite appearances, the excellent health
of the pharmaceutical industry is not a reflection
of its products' quality»

MESSY PRESCRIPTIONS

«The brain is not found under the belt»

«All or nothing»

«Why would I deprive myself?»

I UNDERSTOOD THAT YOU HAD THE SPECIAL LIMITED EDITION MODEL WITH GOLDEN EDGES, PINK INTERIOR AND SILVER BANDS
2351$
MY QUESTION IS: DO YOU HAVE IT WITH PASTEL GREEN EYELETS AND RHINESTONES ON THE ANKLES?
Pyt 22
TOUGH CHOICE

Will we ever be able to say:
«Fire the guns»?

MAKE THE GUNPOWDER TALK

«Please, hurry up in your waiting»

THE RELAXED EMERGENCY

161

«The Art of Giving Consumer Credit»

CLICK & COLLAPSE

Back to the future

ALMOST NATURAL

«I'm afraid of being afraid»

THE FEAR OF EMPTINESS

«Out of date doesn't mean out of hope»

169

«When truth is stranger than fiction»

THE SPIRITUALITY OF PRAGMATISM

«Neighbors Day is delayed to another day
due to a lack of progress»

173

«If you wish to be yourself, please stay with your self»

JUST IN CASE

175

«No matter the uniform or the costume,
the instinct will always wear the pants»

CLOSER TO YOU, MY LORD

Do not mix up

«Guardian angel» and «Mystical warden»

NOT ALONE IN THE WORLD

«The work we embody reflects a deliberate action,
dressed up as a coincidence»

«I want to welcome you well,
but please leave everything you are on the doorstep»

GREAT REPLACEMENT

183

«Ignorance and disdain make a combination whose explosion will be much stronger than the simple addition of the two parts»

RUNNING BEFORE BEING ABLE TO WALK

«The winners make history, losers become conspiracists»

NEWS OR HOAX

«Don't give up until you find the solution,
or you'll end up empty-handed like a dumbass»

«With all my affliction»

QUESTION OF GENDER

«We really have to go through hell to reach heaven»

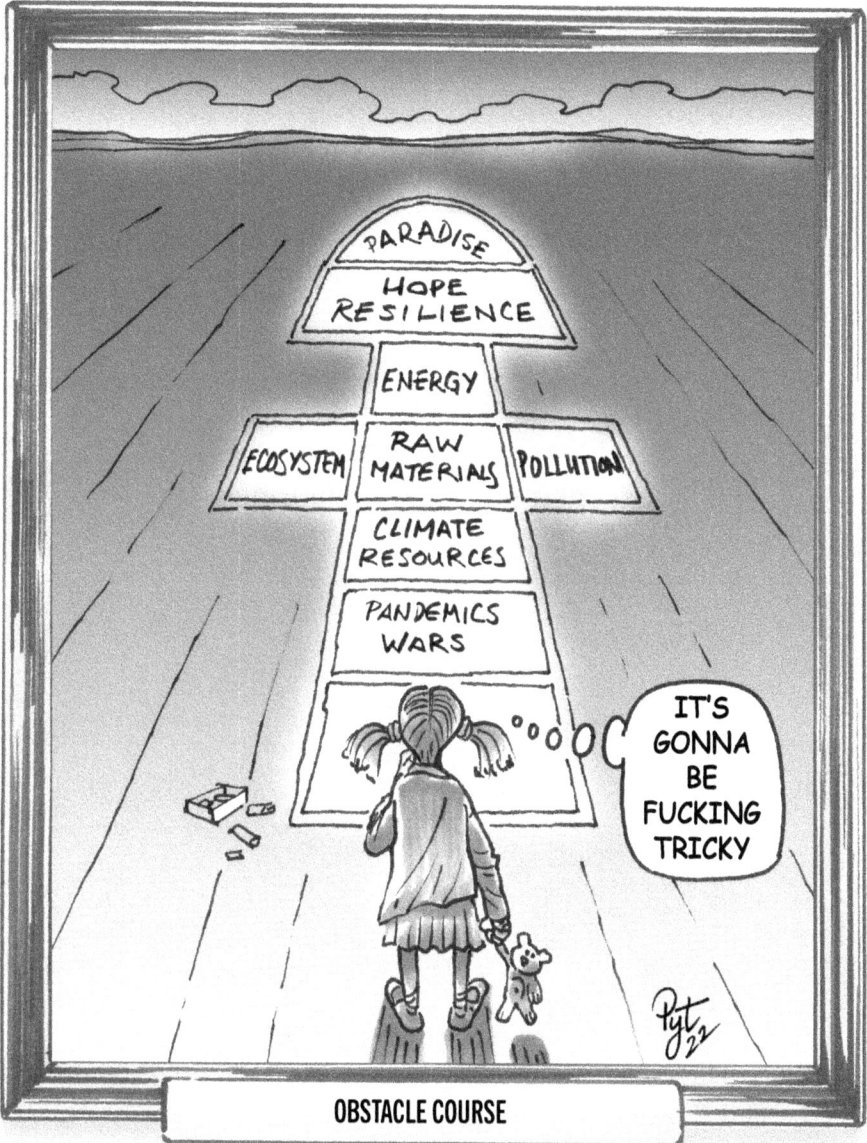

OBSTACLE COURSE

«Tomorrow is another day,
except it might be night time»

«Prevention is better than suffering»

NIPPED IN THE BUD

«Are we talking about a frontal impact between the legs?»

METAPHYSICAL SHORTCUT

«Back to the future, again»

« Keep it up that way and you will not have any desert!»

YOU HAVE BEAUTIFUL DUNES, YOU KNOW

«Respect is earned, but merit is no longer respected»

OUT OF ORDER

«Stock depletion is announced,
but the growing demand is confirmed»

EYES ARE BIGGER THAN THE STOMACH

«It feels so good to harm
that we end up thinking it's right»

DEADLY ARCHITECTURE

pluscontumeurs.com

French & English website

ISBN: 978-2-9550128-3-3

www.ingramcontent.com/pod-product-compliance
Lightning Source LLC
Chambersburg PA
CBHW070329090426
42733CB00012B/2416